BECOMING *creative*   **BECOMING** *thoughtful*   **BECOMING** *strong*

BECOMING *inspired*   **BECOMING** *honest*   **BECOMING** *open*

BECOMING *purposeful*   *driven*   **BECOMING** *creative*

BECOMING *helpful*   **BECOMING** *happy*   **BECOMING** *curious*

BECOMING *secure*   **BECOMING** *thankful*

I AM BECOMING

Your story is what you have,
what you will always have.
It is something to own.

This story belongs to

Becoming
isn't about arriving
somewhere or
achieving a certain
aim. It's forward
motion, a means
of evolving,
a way to reach
continuously
toward a better self.

A NOTE FROM MICHELLE

After my memoir was published, I heard a similar reaction from a lot of people—strangers, friends, and family alike. They said, "I just can't believe you remembered that much." It's a comment that usually gave me a bit of a chuckle, because when I think back to the process of reflecting for my memoir, what I remember most is the feeling of grasping at memories that were just barely out of my reach. *What was her name? Did I make that decision before or after that talk with Barack? Which state was that campaign event in?*

I'd only kept a journal for a short period of my life, for a couple of years during my late twenties as I was getting more serious with Barack and contemplating a new career. It was a tumultuous time filled with change, and I found that dedicating time to writing my thoughts down helped me navigate all the transitions. Then I put it away and didn't pick it up again until I began writing my memoir. Instantly, I was transported back to that earlier version of myself, with all the warmth, heartbreak, and frustration flooding in.

The experience left me asking myself, "Why didn't I journal more?" The answer, like for so many of you, I'm sure, was that I simply got busy. I switched careers. I got married. I had children. Somewhere along the line, I ended up in ball gowns at the White House, however that happened.

Looking back, I wish I'd taken more time to write down what I was thinking and feeling. I didn't journal much because I talked myself out of it—journaling can feel a little intimidating and layered with implication, the idea being that once you put pen to paper, your thoughts have extra weight and meaning.

What I recognize now, though, is far more simple: We don't have to remember everything. But everything we remember has value.

You don't have to write in poetry or wait for some lightning-bolt epiphany. You don't have to journal every day, and you certainly don't have to feel like you have anything important to say. You might write down something as mundane as the sound of an ice scraper on a windshield on a freezing-cold Chicago morning. The whiff of Pine-Sol in the house after spring cleaning. The ride home from the airport in your mother's car. Your to-do list for the next day, even. One of my favorite entries recounted an otherwise uneventful night at a neighborhood restaurant where an old man punched the perfect playlist into a jukebox.

Just remember that everything matters—the sounds and the smells, the laughs and the pain—because in the end, it's all a part of your story. I hope you'll use this journal to write down your experiences, thoughts, and feelings, in all their imperfections, and without judgment. This isn't an exercise to sugarcoat your experiences, or write down something different from what you actually feel, or try to will yourself toward some perfect outcome. Because the beauty of life is that an experience you have today might feel totally different after a few months, or years, or decades. You might return to these pages and recognize parts of yourself that you can't even see today, which is especially true for those of you who are still in the early stages of your journeys, when the joys and hurt can sometimes feel too fresh, too raw. Writing is a way to process, to understand, to grow, and yes, to remember.

That's perhaps the most fundamental part of becoming: seeing this collection of stories that you'll write and embracing them for what they are—yours.

Much love,

Michelle Obama

If you don't see that your story matters, chances are no one else will either. So even though it isn't always easy, it's important for you to find the strength to share your truth. Because the world needs to hear it.

What's your story and
how have you learned
to embrace it?

DATE / /

Where did your story take a sudden turn?

BECOMING

Do you have any favorite quotes? Capture three of them here.

I was raised to be
confident and see
no limits, to believe
I could go after
and get absolutely
anything I wanted.
And I wanted
everything . . .

What do you want? List ten things you want for yourself. For each item, write one simple step toward making that wish come true.

1. _____

2. _____

3. _____

4. _____

5. _____

6. _____

7. _____

8. _____

9. _____

10. _____

Describe your
childhood home.
What are some of
the details that stand
out the most? What
made your home
different from your
friends' homes?

Describe your home today. How is it different from your friends' homes? What do you love about it the most?

I had nothing
or I had everything.
It depends on
which way you
want to tell it.

Where we come from has such a strong effect on the person we are. Describe the neighborhood you grew up in. What was special about it? What was challenging? How did it shape who you are today?

List five favorite family dishes.

1

2

3

4

5

Describe a memorable dinner. What did you eat? Did you eat at home or somewhere else?

BECOMING

What did you do as a
child when school let
out for the summer?

What activities did you
previously pursue but
don't have time for
now? How can you get
back to them again?

BECOMING

If you could have a
conversation with
a loved one who
has passed away,
what would you ask
him or her?

Where did your
ancestors come from
and what challenges
did they face?

BECOMING

If there's one thing I've learned in life, it's the power of using your own voice.

Write about a time when you spoke your truth to others. How did it make you feel? What did you learn?

What kind of person
do you want to
become?

How do you want
to contribute to
the world? What
is one small step
you can take this
year to further that
contribution?

BECOMING

DATE   /   /

Have courage this
month to share a little
more of your story
with someone else.
Ask them about theirs.
What did you learn
about yourself? What
did you learn about
this person?

There's power in allowing yourself to be known and heard, in owning your unique story, in using your authentic voice. And there's grace in being willing to know and hear others. This, for me, is how we become.

What are the greatest
lessons you learned
as a child?

BECOMING

My family
was my world,
the center of
everything.

What does family mean to you?

In as much detail
as possible, capture
one favorite memory
you've created with
your loved ones.

Describe your perfect day—beginning with breakfast and ending with dinner.

DATE / /

Write a letter to your
teenage self, giving
advice and revealing
what the future holds.

Write a letter to your
future self, outlining
your expectations for
the years to come.

BECOMING

What's the most spontaneous thing you have ever done?

DATE   /   /

What were the ten biggest things that happened to you this month?

1. _____

2. _____

3. _____

4. _____

5. _____

6. _____

7. _____

8. _____

9. _____

10. _____

I was female, black,
and strong, which
to certain people,
maintaining a certain
mind-set, translated only
to "angry." It was another
damaging cliché, one
that's been forever used to
sweep minority women
to the perimeter of every
room, an unconscious
signal not to listen to
what we've got to say.

Have you ever felt
subject to a cliché?
How did you react?

BECOMING

Look outside a
window in your home.
Write down what
you see.

What was the biggest
news headline on the
day you were born?
Is it something that is
still relevant today?

What was the last
great book you read?
What did you learn
from it?

One of the first books that I loved and read cover to cover in one day . . . was a book called *Song of Solomon* by Toni Morrison. And that book helped me love reading, because before then reading was kind of like something you did when you had to do it. But that book, it grabbed me and pulled me and I just kept reading and kept reading. . . . There are many, many other books that I've read like that over the years, but *Song of Solomon* was my first one.

List ten fun things you like to do.

1. _____

   _____

2. _____

   _____

3. _____

   _____

4. _____

   _____

5. _____

   _____

6. _____

   _____

7. _____

   _____

8. _____

   _____

9. _____

   _____

10. _____

   _____

What is your most prized possession and how did you come to own it?

BECOMING

Failure is a
feeling long before
it becomes an
actual result.
It's vulnerability
that breeds with
self-doubt and then
is escalated,
often deliberately,
by fear.

What can you do—as an individual, parent, or
community member—to help break a cycle of
fear and failure?

Pick a favorite photo
and write a story
describing what you
see.

Who is the happiest
person you know?
What do you think
brings them joy?

BECOMING

In seeking out
new perspectives
and reaching outside
of our comfort
zones, we can
discover more about
ourselves.

If you could travel anywhere, where would
you go and what would you do?

DATE   /   /

BECOMING

Think back to your
childhood when
you would visit
grandparents or other
elders. Capture one
specific memory from
those visits in the
fullest detail possible,
including the sights,
sounds, and smells.

How have those elders
left a mark on you?

BECOMING

List ten favorite vegetables and how you like to prepare them.

1.

2.

3.

4.

5.

6.

7.

8.

9.

10.

I now knew that
strawberries were at
their most succulent
in June, that darker-
leaf lettuces had the
most nutrients, and
that it wasn't so hard
to make kale chips
in the oven.

How does nature
nourish you?

BECOMING

How do you celebrate
the holidays? What
traditions does your
family hold dear?

Describe a memorable
holiday—whether
recently or in the past.
Where were you? Who
was there? What food
was served?

You don't really
know how attached
you are until you
move away, until
you've experienced
what it means to be
dislodged, a cork
floating on the ocean
of another place.

When were you last flung into new or
uncomfortable terrain? How did this sudden
change affect you? What value did it bring
to your life?

BECOMING

Kids will invest more when they feel they're being invested in.

List five people who invested in you
when you were a child.

Choose one person
from your list on
the opposite page
and describe how
his or her support
manifested in your
accomplishments
today.

How did you get to
school every day when
you were young?

Who was the most influential teacher when you were little? How did this person leave such an impression?

BECOMING

What has been your
greatest sacrifice?

BECOMING

I have a habit that has
sustained me for life:
keeping a close and
high-spirited council of
girlfriends—a safe harbor
of female wisdom.

1

List three people who contribute
to your circle of strength. Next to
each person's name, describe why
he or she is so dependable.

2

3

Create a playlist of ten songs that you could listen to on repeat.

1. _____

_____

2. _____

_____

3. _____

_____

4. _____

_____

5. _____

_____

6. _____

_____

7. _____

_____

8. _____

_____

9. _____

_____

10. _____

_____

Music has
always been
a defining part
of who I've
become.

A BECOMING PLAYLIST

1. "Ain't No Mountain High Enough," Marvin Gaye and Tammi Terrell

2. "The Way You Do the Things You Do," The Temptations

3. "Dancing in the Street," Martha Reeves & the Vandellas

4. "Please, Mr. Postman," The Marvelettes

5. "This Old Heart of Mine (Is Weak for You)," The Isley Brothers

6. "Ain't Nothing Like the Real Thing," Marvin Gaye and Tammi Terrell

7. "Baby Love," The Supremes

8. "It's the Same Old Song," Four Tops

9. "Just My Imagination (Running Away with Me)," The Temptations

10. "Signed, Sealed, Delivered (I'm Yours)," Stevie Wonder

11. "I Heard It Through the Grapevine," Gladys Knight & the Pips

12. "My Guy," Mary Wells

13. "It Takes Two," Marvin Gaye and Kim Weston

14. "I Can't Help Myself (Sugar Pie, Honey Bunch)," Four Tops

15. "Who's Loving You," The Jackson 5

16. "Beauty Is Only Skin Deep," The Temptations

17. "The Tracks of My Tears," Smokey Robinson & the Miracles

18. "For Once in My Life," Stevie Wonder

19. "Baby, I'm for Real," The Originals

20. "Reach Out I'll Be There," Four Tops

21. "What's Going On," Marvin Gaye

22. "Mercy Me (The Ecology)," Marvin Gaye

23. "As," Stevie Wonder

24. "Color," Zhané

25. "I Love Your Smile," Shanice

26. "Treat Her Like a Lady," The Temptations

27. "Zoom," Commodores

28. "The Truth," India.Arie

29. "Didn't Cha Know," Erykah Badu

30. "My Cherie Amour," Stevie Wonder

31. "Woman's World," BJ the Chicago Kid

32. "I'm Coming Out," Diana Ross

33. "Video," India.Arie

34. "Square Biz," Teena Marie

35. "Rhythm of the Night," DeBarge

36. "You and I," Rick James

37. "Someday We'll Be Together," Diana Ross & the Supremes

38. "Feel So Good," Perri

I've learned
that it's harder to
hate up close.

Describe a recent conversation you had
with someone who did not share your history
or perspective. How did you navigate the
conversation?

What kind of
childhood did
your parents or
grandparents have?
How was it different
from and similar to
your own?

BECOMING

Your story is the most
powerful part of who
you are—the struggles,
failures, successes, and
everything in between.
Remember always to stay
open to new experiences
and never let the doubters
get in the way.

List one struggle, one failure, and one success you've encountered in your life. What did you learn from each?

A STRUGGLE:

A FAILURE:

A SUCCESS:

Have you spent time
in the military, or know
someone who has?
What does it mean
to you to serve your
country?

How would you
describe yourself to
someone who does
not know you?

BECOMING

Becoming
requires equal
parts patience
and rigor.

Describe a time when patience and rigor
contributed to your own self-love and growth.

Write about a specific experience when someone dislodged a dream
of yours by trying to lower your expectations. How did it make you feel?
How did you try to overcome that obstacle?

List five ways that person was wrong.

1

2

3

4

5

When was your last
good cry, and how did
you feel afterward?

How do you look after
yourself after you've
had a bad day?

BECOMING

A transition is exactly that— a passage to something new.

What transition are you going through right now? Do you feel ready for it?

What was the best
TV show you saw as
a kid? What are you
watching now?

Who is your favorite
TV show character
and what about them
appeals to you?

Think of an endeavor you recently embarked upon—one which may have felt new, exciting, and perhaps a bit scary. List three of your attributes that made you uniquely qualified for the challenge.

2

3

If you could travel
back in time and
give yourself advice
before you took on
a challenge, what
would you say?

How have your beliefs
changed over the
years? How have they
remained the same?

BECOMING

Reflect on your
greatest struggle.
What was it and
how did you grow
from it?

BECOMING

Everyone on
earth is carrying
around an unseen
history, and that
alone deserves some
tolerance.

What major historical events affected your
family—whether in the distant past or more
recently?

What role does
religion or spirituality
play in your life?

Write about a time
when you felt carefree.

Am
I good
enough?

Yes
I am.

List ten reasons you are a special and worthy person. Look back at this list whenever you are in doubt. You are always good enough!

1. _____

_____

2. _____

_____

3. _____

_____

4. _____

_____

5. _____

_____

6. _____

_____

7. _____

_____

8. _____

_____

9. _____

_____

10. _____

_____

Write a thank-you
letter to someone
you love.

How do you connect
with your community?

BECOMING

Describe your community and how it has evolved over the past decade.

List five changes you wish a civic leader would take on that would greatly affect your community for the better.

1

2

3

4

5

List your greatest gifts. Remember to embrace them and lay them on the table with pride!

1.

2.

3.

4.

5.

6.

7.

8.

9.

10.

How do you define the word *leader*? Have you ever considered taking on a
leadership role? Why or why not?

BECOMING

Self-doubt doesn't make the feelings any less difficult in the moment, but in the end, it can actually be useful, as long as we don't let it overwhelm the way we think about ourselves.

What worries about yourself have you had that proved to be untrue? What methods do you use when faced with self-doubt?

So many of us go
through life with
our stories hidden,
feeling ashamed
or afraid when our
whole truth doesn't
live up to some
established ideal . . .
That is, until
someone dares to
start telling that
story differently.

Describe someone you know who was brave enough to tell their story. How did it change your perception of them? How did it change your perception of yourself?

How do you mark the
seasons? What is your
favorite month of the
year?

Do you embrace
change in your own
life? Why or why not?

BECOMING

To me,
the magic is in
the learning.

What skills or lessons have you sought
to learn as an adult? How does learning
bring about change in your life today?

BECOMING

What trailblazer
throughout history
has shaped you the
most? If you could
meet this person,
what questions
would you ask?

BECOMING

What legacy do you
want to leave behind?

We were planting
seeds of change, the
fruit of which we
might never see. We
had to be patient.

List five tiny victories you accomplished this week.

1

2

3

4

5

Change happens from the ground up. What is one small thing you can do this week to bring about new change in your life or in the life of someone else?

BECOMING

If you don't get out there and define yourself, you'll be quickly and inaccurately defined by others.

How have others tried to define you in the past and how do their perceptions differ from the person you know you are?

Write about someone
outside your family
who feels like a family
member. What do you
love about them the
most?

BECOMING

The important parts
of my story, I was
realizing, lay less in
the surface value of my
accomplishments and
more in what undergirded
them—the many small
ways I'd been buttressed
over the years, and the
people who'd helped build
my confidence over time.

Who are your mentors and how do you cultivate
those relationships?

How often do you get together with your friends, and what do you like to do? Is it enough?

List your ten favorite movies.

1. _____

2. _____

3. _____

4. _____

5. _____

6. _____

7. _____

8. _____

9. _____

10. _____

How do you give back
to your community?

How have you been
able to create change
in the lives of other
people?

BECOMING

If you were asked to give a commencement speech, what advice would you offer the graduates?

What happened in your life today? List five things that went well.

1

2

3

4

5

DATE / /

What does self-care
mean to you? How
can you make more
time for taking care
of yourself?

Who do you care for
in your family? How
does that relationship
help define you?

Coexisting with
Barack's strong sense
of purpose . . .
was something
to which I had to
adjust, not because
he flaunted it,
exactly, but because
it was so alive.

What gives you purpose? Who else in your life
shares your resolve?

Have you experienced
loss? How did it shape
your life?

Write about the
last moment you
remember being truly
at peace. Where were
you? What were you
doing? How can you
tap into that feeling
again?

BECOMING

When is the last time you felt you might be on the wrong path even though the world thought you were doing exactly the right thing? What did you decide to do?

List the ten most important social issues you feel need attending to.

1. _____

2. _____

3. _____

4. _____

5. _____

6. _____

7. _____

8. _____

9. _____

10. _____

When they go low, we go high.

How do you put this phrase into practice?

Who was your first
love?

How does your family
handle the pressures
of the outside world?

Have you ever
embraced ambitions
that put you at odds
with the people
you love and trust
the most? How did
you straddle those
different worlds?

If you could find more
time to do what you love,
what would you do?

I wanted to have a
work life and a home life,
but with some promise
that one would never fully
squelch the other.
I hoped to be exactly like
my own mother and
at the same time nothing
like her at all. It was an
odd and confounding
thing to ponder.
Could I have everything?
Would I have everything?
I had no idea.

How do you balance
the competing worlds
of your home life and
work life?

List ten outings you've been on with your family.

1. _____

2. _____

3. _____

4. _____

5. _____

6. _____

7. _____

8. _____

9. _____

10. _____

Pick one outing from your list and dig a little deeper: what did you do, where did you go, and who went with you?

BECOMING

Who or what are you
grateful for?

How do you express
your gratitude?

BECOMING

When have you had to
swerve in life? How did
it help you?

How do you stay
centered?

BECOMING

What is your favorite way to unwind from a particularly demanding day?

What inspires you? List the first ten things that come to mind.

1. _____

2. _____

3. _____

4. _____

5. _____

6. _____

7. _____

8. _____

9. _____

10. _____

The most successful
people I know have
figured out how to
live with criticism,
to lean on the people
who believe in them,
and to push onward
with their goals.

Reflect on one person you know who has
overcome obstacles to accomplish their goals.
How do you think they did it? What have you
learned from their journey?

BECOMING

Describe a time when
you had to speak up
for yourself. What gave
you the courage? What
stood in your way?

Have you ever felt
the need to speak
up for someone else?
Describe the situation
and the outcome.

BECOMING

Who is your role
model? How has that
person shaped you?

Who looks up to you?
How do you nurture
that person's spark?

BECOMING

What's the best part of your morning routine?

List five things you do to unwind from the day.

1

2

3

4

5

Capture a favorite
family recipe here.
How is it unique?

Where did your name
come from and how
has it influenced
the person you've
become?

BECOMING

How do you bring
your own history,
culture, and
experiences into
spaces where they
never existed?

If you could rewrite
history books, what
would you add that
was left out?

DATE   /   /

Describe the world
of your dreams. What
changes—whether
on a local, national,
or global level—do
you wish to see?

People of all
backgrounds, skin
colors, and political
persuasions can relate
to feeling uncertain
or overwhelmed.
We've all been a little
frustrated by the slow,
frustrating growth
necessary to get
where we want to go.

Describe a specific
place that holds
important meaning
to your family.

If you had to choose, who is the most precious person in your life? How did you meet this person and what do you think your future together holds?

BECOMING

What were five books you loved as a child?

1

2

3

4

5

Describe someone in your life who is truly wise.

BECOMING

Use this space to write
a letter to someone
you haven't seen in a
long time, updating
him or her on what's
happened in your
life since you last saw
each other.

Use this space to
capture your favorite
family sayings along
with who said them
and what they mean
to you.

BECOMING

In my life so far,
I'd worn very few
gowns, but Jason
Wu's creation
performed a potent
little miracle,
making me feel soft
and beautiful and
open again, just as I
began to think I had
nothing of myself
left to show.

List ten items of clothing you loved along with when and where you wore them.

1. _____

_____

2. _____

_____

3. _____

_____

4. _____

_____

5. _____

_____

6. _____

_____

7. _____

_____

8. _____

_____

9. _____

_____

10. _____

_____

Education has
been the primary
instrument of
change in my own
life, my lever upward
in the world.

What role has education—whether formal or
informal—played in your life?

In as much detail as possible, describe one of your favorite childhood memories.

List ten things you noticed on your way home today that no one else may
have noticed.

1. _____

_____

2. _____

_____

3. _____

_____

4. _____

_____

5. _____

_____

6. _____

_____

7. _____

_____

8. _____

_____

9. _____

_____

10. _____

_____

Spend an evening
or afternoon without
looking at social
media or the news.
How did it feel to
unplug even for just a
short amount of time?

When your extended
family gets together,
what do you do?

I was lucky to have parents, teachers, and mentors who'd fed me with a consistent, simple message:

You matter.

Who makes you feel like you matter? How do they let you know?

What do you like to do to stay healthy?

List three new hobbies you'd like to learn to do. What about each of them appeals to you?

My father loved any excuse to drive. He was devoted to his car, a bronze-colored two-door Buick Electra 225, which he referred to with pride as "the Deuce and a Quarter."

Describe your family car or other mode of transportation you took as a child. Capture the sounds and smells.

What's the longest
road trip you've ever
been on?

DATE   /   /

What would make
your neighborhood a
better place?

DATE   /   /

Kids know at a very young age when they're being devalued.

How do you make the children in your life feel valued?

What keeps you up at
night?

How has this year
been different from
last year?

DATE   /   /

What five things do you want to have accomplished by the end of the month?

1

2

3

4

5

Close this journal, shut your eyes, and take ten deep breaths. Write down how you feel.

BECOMING

Think of a time when
you gave away some-
thing you loved. What
did you give away
and why?

DATE   /   /

When was the last
time you saw the
sunset? What were you
doing at the time?

BECOMING

Becoming is never
giving up on the idea
that there's more
growing to be done.

What does the idea of "becoming" mean to you?

VIKING

UK | USA | Canada | Ireland | Australia
India | New Zealand | South Africa

Viking is part of the Penguin Random House group of companies
whose addresses can be found at global.penguinrandomhouse.com.

Penguin
Random House
UK

First published in the United States of America by Clarkson Potter/Publishers,
an imprint of Random House, a division of Penguin Random House LLC, New York
First published in Great Britain by Viking 2019
001

Selected material originally appeared in *Becoming* by Michelle Obama,
first published in the United States of America by Crown, an imprint of Penguin
Random House LLC, New York, in 2018, and first published in Great Britain
by Viking in 2018

Design by Danielle Deschenes

Printed in Italy by Printer Trento S.r.l.

A CIP catalogue record for this book is available from the British Library

ISBN: 978—0—241—44415—3

BECOMING
brave

BECOMING
passionate

BECOMING
kind

BECOMING
happy

BECOMING
curious

BECOMING
grateful

BECOMING
bold

secure

BECOMING
strong

BECOMING
honest

BECOMING
inspired

BECOMING
accepting

BECOMING
open

daring

BECOMING
grateful